For operators in business and social economy

English edition 001:
Me and my secretary

Berlin 2019

Me and my secretary
Communication and company culture

The proof of the pudding ... Welcome in real life ...

SPRUNGBRETT zum
€RFOLG

SCHULUNGS- & BERATUNGSGESELLSCHAFT

Bernd Jaenicke

Acknowledgements:

I want to thank my son, Isonga Bernd, who has given valuable support regarding the layout, the concept and the practical realisation of this topical series at amazon.de and gave useful feedback, input and implemented the publication of this series.

Translations from German into English:

Helle Kuhlenkamp, translations and company services
https://www.helle-kuhlenkamp.de

An apology in advance:

The author is a male person and had had various secretaries in the course of his working life. The author writes from his own perspective and experience. Naturally, the executive may also be a female person, and her secretary the opposite. Naturally, there are various possible gender constellations between executives and their staff. The author takes the liberty to write from his own experience and offers a sincere apology in advance.

Me and my secretary
Communication and company culture

What it is about:

Few relationships can be more complex and complicated than the one between an executive and his secretary (or, of course, between an executive and her secretary) No wonder, when you are a man and she a woman (or the exact opposite) and you spend more time with your secretary and maybe travel more with him or her than with your wife or husband.

This proximity creates a field of tension which has to be addressed: The way you handle your secretary and how you communicate with each other will set an example for company culture and for the other staff.

To engage in positive and constructive communication will set a more valid example than all well-meant appeals.

Me and my secretary
Communication and company culture

Contents

Me and my secretary
Communication and company culture

1. INTRODUCTION

The quality of your relationship with the secretary can have far-reaching impact on other, various aspects, even if you will not always notice it during your day-to-day work. Work pressure, deadlines, personnel issues and problems often don't allow for time to develop and 'work on' the relationship to your secretary. Conflictual relationships can impact various work processes, entrepreneurial success and, last but not least, your married life.

Serious tensions can cause considerable, daily strain felt on both sides. This can be tedious, cost time and energy, and may destroy motivation for the daily work. Your interaction affects, in a positive or negative way, the entire corporate culture. It sets a precedent and is a model for the other employees of your company.

Often, the small details regulate and shape the kind of relationship you have, and lead to certain, deep-rooted types of behaviour, which will then be perceived as 'normal.' From your secretary's side, there could be signs of small power struggles ('Remember that I will go for break at 1p.m.'), craving for recognition ('Nobody ever listens to me') or of knowing it all ('I told you so, last week') open or covert insinuations (' Your tie and your shirt, perfectly colour-coordinated'), little capacity to work under pressure ('I can't do everything at once!') personal sensitivities, which are conveyed verbally or non-verbally to others, ('Do not talk to me about it') or the wish to change decisions you made ('Wouldn't it be better if we...') to show only a few examples.

The difference between a constructive and destructive behaviour may sometimes only lie in her delivery: ('Did you iron these pants'?) The sentence could be irreverent and reproachful, but can also mean that she tells you, in a friendly, motherly way, that it could be better (but is still okay). Often, such small details make a difference.

For example:
You are in a hurry and need to give your secretary a piece of information before you go. But our secretary is talking on the telephone. Does she react to your request? Does she interrupt her call for a moment? Does she react at all when spoken to while on the telephone? These are not really small matters. These are power issues that need to be addressed and corrected.

The examples from daily practice are many, and not all tensions or power struggles are carried out in a subliminal way. An intelligent and destructive-minded secretary can cost a lot of energy and considerably impede the daily work-flow.

Tip 1:
If you do not proactively shape and steer the relationship,
your secretary will do the steering.

---

2.   YOUR SECRETARY

2.1.   YOUR SECRETARY EXERTS INFLUENCE

Your secretary probably knows all company processes, members of staff, customers, other companies and persons better than you. And she knows you, with all your strengths and weaknesses, better than all co-workers, customers, firm partners and other persons. In many processes, within and outside the company, she is a filter you need to use.

Executive

⇕

How does she filter information?

⇕

Co-workers Customers Partners Others

Whereas you, according to your position, have more formal and business-like relations to people inside and outside your company, your secretary will be able to maintain personal and confident contacts. Therefore, she will also know more about the peculiarities or weaknesses of the staff members.

This gives her a position of considerable strength. She will uphold this position, among other things, by filtering or selecting information and will not tell you everything she hears. By this, she will gain the confidence of co-workers, customers and business partners.

An example:
If the performance of a certain staff member has changed for the worse due to alcohol abuse, you will usually be the last to know (either from a staff member or from the secretary) The same rule applies for many other areas.

Leave your secretary in her powerful position, do not make her tell all about it and observe how she makes use of her responsibility . You don't have to know every little thing going on in the company. You will only need to hear the important facts and those must be presented to you confidentially by your secretary.

Your secretary knows:
- Your employees better than you
- Your customers and business partners better and more personal than you
- Many internal work-flows and "hacks"
- Your peculiarities, strengths and weaknesses better than others.

Your secretary has:
- Confidential information about the company
- Confidential information about the staff
- Confidential information from staff
- Confidential information about your business and private life.

Your secretary exerts influence over:
-        The employees
-        Your image among your employees
-        Your assessment of others
-        Your customers
-        Your business partners
-        and, most of all, over you.

Hardly any other member of the staff wields such a far-reaching influence. Thus, the secretary usually holds a special and powerful position within the company.   A responsible and disciplined use of these opportunities to influence others is not easy and demands special skills.

The scope of influence, and the use of internal or confidential information by your secretary, reaches from steady, reliable support and valuable support to an extreme, conflictual, time-intensive interference, harmful for company processes and business development.

Depending on her actual tasks, the secretary has to assume various roles: She is your employee, but also a colleague, she conveys company instructions and acts as an intermediary between all participators in the business. First of all, she should stand loyally to you, but also act as trusted agent for you and the employees alike.

An example:
Your secretary shall hand over a letter of warning, set up by you, to an employee. Does she hand over the letter without comment? Does she tell the staffer that she has tried to dispel the warning, or that he/she had it coming? You cannot know what your secretary says when handing over the letter, or afterwards. The example illustrates, however, that the secretary can use confidential information in a positive or negative way.

Tip 2:
Your secretary has access to confidential information
from various sources and she exerts influence.
Listen to her.

C.   OBSERVE "FROM A DISTANCE"

It can be very useful to observe the actors involved, their practices, their forms of communication, their strengths and weaknesses, their sometimes destructive ability to deliver subtexts or insinuations, their manipulative techniques, lack of work-related clarity or discipline from as far a distance as possible. The actors involved are you and your secretary.

C.1.   OBSERVE YOURSELF

Do you deliberately shape the relationship with your secretary? How do you behave towards her? How and when are you checking on her? Where do you feel trustful, where mistrustful about her? When and how do you give criticism? When and how do you give positive feedback? How much personal proximity do you want to allow? How strict are you? How transparent are your instructions? How clear are your expectations? How do you handle conflict?

An example:
You have seen a real nice joke while reading the newspaper during break and want to tell it to your secretary. By doing this, you did more than telling a joke. In fact, you have shaped a part of the verbal culture between both. Telling jokes will be now 'okay', and your secretary can, sooner or later, also tell you a funny story.

C.2.   OBSERVE YOUR SECRETARY

Is your secretary aware of her particular position? Does she use it responsibly? Does she sometimes take advantage of it? How does she talk about you to others? Does she strengthen your position against others? For which kind of co-workers would she advocate? Which co-workers or which groups of co-workers does she meet during breaks? With which co-workers does she have personal contact? Are you generally accepted by all staffers she has personal contact with? Does she know the limits of her responsibilities? How does she handle conflicts? How does your secretary assess you? Which kind of evaluation would she give about you? What are her strengths and weaknesses?

An example:
Your secretary tells one of the co-workers that you made some spelling mistake, e.g. that you wrote 'tinfoyl' again. Such statements are mostly not objective claims about your orthography, but hint at a partly or entirely negative attitude towards you and convey to colleagues a negative impression of your abilities.

C.3.   OBSERVE YOUR RELATIONSHIP

How familiar, how detached is your contact? Is there a general, mutual feeling of professional and personal respect? Are there issues 'hanging in the air,' that are not addressed? Which open or hidden conflicts are there? Do you have techniques for resolving or reducing them? Which peculiarities, open or hidden interactions take place between you?

An example:
Your secretary tells one of the co-workers that you made some spelling mistake, e.g. that you wrote 'tinfoyl' again. Did you put it to her clearly how it will cause a negative impression among co-workers, that it conveys a more fundamental criticism of you and that she, the secretary alone, is responsible for correct spelling?

You are not required to take part in a spelling bee. You are required to lead a firm or to head a department. Through giving dictation for reports and letters, some CEOs and managers forget rules of spelling. A good secretary knows this and will not make such remarks.

Tip 3:
Observe your behaviour, the behaviour of your secretary and
the way you interact with each other.

D.   CONFLICTS AND RELATIONS

There is no relationship free of conflict. Even more when the relationship is close. This applies to private and business relationships alike. Despite that, there is often little practical knowledge about conflict solution strategies and little courage to address conflicts. Even though conflicts are a strain on relationships, time and energy, they are often put aside without resolution. Many managers or CEOs have learned how to solve operational and administrative problems effectively in a professional way. Confronted with HR issues, they tend to act a bit on the awkward side. This is just normal. Psychologists or pedagogues will, conversely, not often become managers or heads of companies. Each professional sector has special skills, and nobody is perfect.

Small and middle businesses do, however, depend very much on the reliability of their staff. Manager and bosses should not only manage the business, but also their employees and especially the secretary.

## D.1.	CONFLICTS

Unregarded, undisputed and unresolved conflicts will not be forgotten, they accumulate until the famous 'last straw.' Often a veritable heap of conflicts accrues, which will be, at that date, almost impossible to solve. The tensions will then erupt at the smallest provocation, often into unchecked aggression or fits of rage. Badly maintained relationships, neglected for years, are hard to repair.

To solve a conflict does not always mean that it is truly resolved, in the sense of completely sorted out. To solve a conflict can also mean to address it, but without finding a solution. It can mean that the different points of view have been expressed. It can also mean that a clear work instruction has be given. It is important to acknowledge a conflict and /or come to an internally constructive solution with the persons concerned. Conflicts that have already been regarded, are generally less onerous and can become smaller or even insignificant. The different views and expectations, if they are expressed openly, can be generally handled by most people. Naturally, each rule or instruction that is neither understood nor accepted, can trigger fresh conflicts.

In any case, the real cause for conflicts must be found, if they are not yet defined. Very often, new conflicts arise because the old ones have not been resolved.

For example:
Today, your secretary leaves the office, although there are still things to do, contrary to normal habit at 5 pm. on the dot due to an 'important' private appointment. On the next day, there will be a 'talk' or debate regarding the question when and where working after 5 pm will be required.

But the reason for her behaviour was not her private appointment, but rather an argument from the day before. If the real conflicts cannot be defined, or addressed, new ones can emerge without having 'got rid' of the old ones. This way, problems are building up more and more.

Tip 4:
There is no relationship free of conflict.
Conflicts put aside can re-emerge somewhere else,
without recognizable the context.

## D.2.	RELATIONS

Seen from the male perspective, most relationships to women recall a relation to a mother, a daughter or a wife. The relationship of a male executive to his secretary is no exception. The 'classification' however, is not only determined by age groups but also by the way you both 'agree', often implicitly, to interact.

All types of relationships mentioned above share a well-known problem. The more personal proximity to your secretary you allow, the more your wife or partner will 'prick up her ears'. There will be hardly any woman who will not harbour general feelings of jealousy towards her husbands' secretary and who would not remember what you said about yours. Statistics about amorous relationships between a boss and his secretary will basically show she has a point, until you can, by your behaviour, not by statements, prove her wrong.

The 'father-daughter-relationship' or the 'mother-son' kind have the additional risk to exaggerate some aspects of your roles or to become stuck in a certain constellation. This can be difficult for you and your secretary alike.

Generally, none of the kinds described above are better, more difficult or more recommendable than others. Each form of relationships has its advantages and its conflicts.

The less conflictual relation, however, is the 'working relationship'. This means a relationship which is, as far as possible, defined by a disciplined, friendly and constructive working on daily tasks and limits private matters to occasional polite questions like 'How is the family' (with possible answers like: 'Thanks' or 'Our daughter had measles').

No relationship is 'peculiar' or arbitrary. Each relationship has a history of development. In the course of it, the persons concerned will have 'agreed' to things and regulated and 'normalized' the relationship in a positive or negative way.

Those agreements do not only emerge by outspoken expectations, instructions or arrangements. To a greater degree, people 'agree' on things

      a.   by silence
      b.   by body language
      c.   by their behaviour.

You 'agree' by silence, if you do not confront the other and not speak out if his/her behaviour is inappropriate or undesirable. Agreement by silence can also mean that you give assent by not mentioning expectations you have of the other. To declare expectations as 'self-evident' will not suffice. Expectations should be clear and outspoken.

'Agreeing' by body language means the (mutual) use of positive, negative, sympathetic, angry, or mocking facial expressions, gestures and movements, to mention some examples. The options for positive and negative assessments or reactions by body language can be as varied as the spoken word.

Agreement by your own behaviour means to set-especially as an executive-precedents by your own actions and appearance as a pattern for positive or negative interaction.

As I already said, to 'agree on' does not necessary mean that all persons concerned like certain behaviours or working methods. Often, the opposite can be true. To 'agree' in our sense means that the quality or type of relationships, and working behaviour, is regulated and practised as part of a daily routine.

> **For example:**
> Many standard letters are written autonomously by your secretary and are only submitted for signature. The letters are always factually and grammatically correct, but do not meet your standards of politeness and a friendly, personalized address. You have been displeased with this for a long time and often react angry and annoyed. Your secretary will always say things like: 'It is only a short message' or 'There wasn't much time' or, maybe: 'This is unnecessary in a business letter.' The example shows that you have already 'agreed' on the fact that she is not always polite enough and that you will dislike that.

E.   YOU SHAPE THE RELATIONSHIP

If you do not shape the relationship proactively, your secretary will. Even if you do not like some parts of the bargain, you have given your assent by not making objections.

E.1.   METHODS TO SHAPE THE RELATIONSHIP

There are many possibilities to leave the development of relations not to chance, but to shape them in a proactive way. The most important ways to do this are shortly described in the following:

E.1.1.   BY YOUR OWN EXAMPLE

The first commandment for developing the relationship is to be exemplary in your own conduct . Your way of working, your methods, your conduct and behaviour define company culture and act as a pattern, not only for your secretary. The aspired culture should be work-orientated, friendly and respectful in tone, but clear and unambiguous in content.

E.1.2.   BY CLEAR INSTRUCTIONS

Instructions and expectations regarding work and conduct should be given clearly and unambiguously. Unambiguous and clear instructions and regulations give your secretary security about her own conduct. By doing this, your secretary will know where limits are, which tone and which working methods are desired and required.

E.1.3.   BY ACKNOWLEDGING CONFCLICTS

Problems and conflicts must not be pushed aside. They need to be recognized, or, even better, addressed. In these cases, avoid all avoidance. Conflicts need to be put 'on the table' and solutions, or partial solutions, have to be actively and constructively sought. Conflicts limit in scope as soon as they become recognized and regarded, even if no solution can be found at the moment.

E.1.4.   BY TALKING ABOUT REMARKS, SAYINGS, FACIAL EXPRESSIONS AND GESTURES

The same as in the previous paragraph applies to all forms of negative or harmful talk, sayings, gestures and facial expressions. Although you should not enter a lengthy discussion about it. This can cause more confusion and opens the door for adept talkers. Most negative or damaging forms of behaviour are rather explicit and do not require lengthy debates.

> **For example:**
> In an American company, co-workers greet each other on Fridays as a matter of principle with the abbreviation: 'TGIF'. The abbreviation stands for: 'Thank God, it´s Friday'. This means that working all week has been hell and all look forward to the heaven of weekend. Even if the persons concerned are not really aware of it, such sayings still support a basically negative attitude towards work.

E.1.5.   BY CLARIFYING MISUNDERSTANDINGS

Misunderstandings result from a lack of clarity. The fewer 'chemistry' between people, the more misunderstandings. Or the other way round, the better people get along with each other, the fewer misunderstandings they have. Be that as it may, misunderstandings have to be clarified. This often takes a little time. If there are more and more misunderstandings, one of the persons concerned has not spoken clearly enough.

E.1.6.   THROUGH CHALLENGES

Challenge your secretary and put her under strain. Teach her to cope with stress, or even better, to regard stress not as stress but as part of a fulfilled workday. Work can be fun, if you have the right attitude. In a positive atmosphere, a busy workday will not tire you out.

E.1.7.   THROUGH MEANINGFUL FEEDBACK

Praise and encourage your secretary about the things she is really good at - but only about them. This motivates her working behaviour and often also increases the quality of other areas of work, where she isn't that good.

E.1.8.   BY THE EXCLUSION OF ALL PRIVATE MATTERS

Private matters should be banned from the company. Conflicts can always arise when private matters and things are allowed. The fewer employees you have, the bigger the risk of engaging with their private matters. Private matters include, for example, the bringing of private working equipment, pets and other things. Private matters can also mean the 'airing' of private sensitivities.

The 'bad mood' for example, impedes fruitful cooperation. The 'bad mood' is a signal that you do not want to communicate. Employees are, however, paid for doing their work, and this includes in many areas, a readiness to communicate.

E.1.9.   THROUGH YOUR STRENGTHS

Have the strength to admit to your weaknesses and to acknowledge mistakes you made. This can boost your reputation with your secretary and the staff in a big way, because 'nobody is perfect'.

E.1.10.   BY CONSTRUCTIVE BEHAVIOUR

When you discover operational disturbances or mistakes, try not to look for the person who made them, look first for a constructive solution of the problem or a method for limiting the ensuing damage. By doing this, the possible damage will be found and corrected earlier and you will show that your main interest lies in the failure-free operation, rather than individual errors or animosities. Moreover, you will probably have don't have to look for the person who caused the damage. If the corporate culture is sound, he/she will approach you and apologize. You can learn from mistakes. Still: Mistakes should not be repeated.

E.1.11.   BY ELIMINATING OLD CONFLICTS

The old problems or conflicts which have not been addressed have to be recognized, even if there are by now only limited solutions. The fact that they are recognized at all will be regarded as a positive move.

E.1.12.   BY LEADING AND STEERING

The more actively you steer, set rules and precedents, the more clearly you define work and social behaviour and the attitude towards the company, the more clarity and effectivity you will gain in the workday and your daily efforts, internally and externally.

E.1.13.   WITHOUT EMPATHIZING WITH HER SITUATION

Do not expect empathy, either from your secretary or from other employees, for your situation. Your experiences when you start (or lead) a company are often intransparent to the staffers.

E.1.14.   WITHOUT EXPECTING LESS CONFLICT

Do not expect a reduction regarding conflicts and/or problems. This is not what it's about. The point is to find solutions for respective conflicts, so that they will not be a negative influence for months or even years, and to avoid an accrual of conflicts towards a destructive 'explosion'. Since you are in motion, you will encounter conflicts.

Tip 5:
You need to 'work' on the relationship, meaning:
Define, recognize, plan, lead and instruct.

In the following, I want to cover further areas where you can shape working and social behaviour.

E.2.   THE JOB INTERVIEW

The first unrealistic expectations, false signals, prejudices and also general rules for the type of relationship between you and your secretary are created and set during the job interview. Very often, these interviews are not well-prepared and deal predominantly with professional qualifications and operational demands.

Behavioural skills in a company environment or, for example, skills in the handling of confidential information, multitasking or other aforementioned skills can often not be scanned and discovered. There are, of course, no certificates about this and the informative value of the handed-in references is limited.

So, most people must rely on the personal impression gained from a short job interview. Of course, this impression can be wrong.

Why don't ask about personal weaknesses and the readiness to correct them, or why some weaknesses are harder to correct than others? The applicant will either not tell you about real weaknesses or not be aware having such. The weaknesses she names will be mostly insignificant. Asking such questions is not negative. They paint a picture and tell you how much the applicant will be able to adapt to new situations and new environments.

The less standardized, and the more individual the interview is done, the more probable is that it stays memorable, even among many other interviews. For the applicant, the talk has been one of few interviews and they can, as a rule, remember it, even later on, quite well.

There is hardly anything more difficult than finding the right person for the job at hand. Conducting professional job interviews needs special preparation and is a special topic which cannot be covered within this article's scope.

The realization that you selected the wrong secretary, however, will not be very helpful when the interview took place a long time ago and problems are accumulating in the present.

E.3.   THE COMPANY CULTURE

A constructive and work-orientated relationship should be developed not only between you and your secretary. The same culture should be built internally in the company and externally towards your customers. Constructive and positive thinking may be introduced from the top down, but it can be also proactively learnt.

Quote:
'If you want to build a ship, don't gather men collect wood, give out tasks and divide work, but teach them a longing for the sea.'

Antoine de Saint-Exupéry
(Author of: 'The little Prince')

This quote shall show that your secretary does not only need to write polite letters and to have other, technical skills. She also should identify with the company, love her work and find her professional fulfilment in it. A positive general attitude like that, however, does not come at once. It must be taught and developed.

Friendliness, positive thinking and a constructive behaviour should belong to a modern-day corporate concept. Friendly and motivated co-workers achieve more, and your customers will come to appreciate this attitude very much. Think of the difference, still noticeable two years ago, between airline service and customer skills and that of Deutsche Bahn. The difference was not accidental, the airlines had a concept. And, by now, the Deutsche Bahn has changed their concept too.

For example:
When you call a large company nowadays, a friendly voice will answer. 'Hello, company XY here, my name is Maria Schultze, what can I do for you?' Even if these announcements sometimes sound a bit artificial, it is much better than calling the city administration or revenue office and to hear: 'Müller...' At first, you do not know if you are talking to a private individual or a public official at an authority-and if so, which authority.

Despite that, the tone while saying 'Müller' often tells you already if you are connected to a friendly individual voice or a public authority. Public officials often sound like: 'Müller...what do you want?' or Müller here...You're distracting me.'

The outside image of your company, for your customers, is closely linked to the mode of behaviour within.

In your company, however, during the daily work, you will not be able to regulate all facets of the process by friendliness and transparence alone. The treatment of the topics 'Proximity and distance' Trust and Control' 'Special positions and privilege' Praise and reprimand' and 'Assessment,' which are central issues, shall be addressed shortly in the following.

```
Tip 7:
Friendliness is part of the corporate concept.
Or: 'It's not what you say, but how you say it.'
```

E.4.   PROXIMITY AND DISTANCE

It is impossible to avoid proximity altogether, but each form of personal closeness has risks and the possibility of abuse. By too much proximity, many people struggle to maintain necessary discipline. Too much closeness entices people to share very private things in the course of working relationships, which can be a burden and can lead to conflict.

Without any proximity, you will not be able to avoid an image of aloofness and inaccessibility. Such an extreme detachment may prevent the building of trustful relationships. By doing this, you also renege important information that can be important for business and HR decisions.

The line between closeness and distance depends on the position of the respective employees, but, of course, also on the 'personal chemistry' between people. Inevitably, you will keep less distance to your secretary and your substitute and towards employees who can handle proximity sensibly and responsibly than towards others.

It is important that you and nobody else determine the degree of proximity and distance. The degree should not be defined by chance or a domineering employee. You alone should define and state, according to corporate requirements, how much nearness or distance is expected and required.

Generally speaking, a work-orientated, intense and constructive proximity with a clear and unambiguous personal distance is to be aspired. In case of doubt, opt for bit more distance rather than too much proximity.

The modern 'du'-address should be avoided, because it induces the employee to behave in unprofessional ways and is easily misunderstood.

As is often the case, a healthy medium is best, but not always easy to define. Where the limit in each special, different case shall be, cannot be found in any textbook.

E.5.   TRUST AND CONTROL

Everybody knows the quote by W.I. Lenin: 'Trust is good, control is better' Of course, not everything he passed on must be valid, else your company probably wouldn't exist. But this saying, also meaning 'Trust but verify' remains.

Since most mistakes are made not by design, but by accident, all important areas and performance should be subject to control, so that the outcome may be failure-free. This should happen while making clear what kinds of controls take place. The measures must be part of company procedure. Modern quality management methods ensure that control measures seldom cause problems or a loss of trust with employees. In those areas, checking is not really about trust but only to grant quality of outcome.

Problems normally arise, when there are check-ups outside of a fixed and established frame. The reasons for such controls can be varied. It is important that, e.g. all new or special instructions, procedure etc., type and scope of controls will be part of the brief. The employees are then prepared for these measures. Such check-ups are not seen as mistrustful, because everybody makes mistakes and the company, with its employees, must prevent these.

The more the controls are a part of company procedure, the fewer areas remain where you need to rely only on others, and on trust, to get the work done.

Areas which cannot or should not be monitored will exist in every company. In this case, a culture of trust shall be developed which ensures that employees handle tasks to satisfaction without controls. For reasons of time alone, you will be unable to monitor all areas of work.

Control measures during small and simple steps, standard procedure or other tasks which have no standard monitoring procedure can cause in employees the feeling that their performance is disregarded, i.e. giving an impression of mistrust in the person's abilities. Such misjudgements are highly demotivating.

Where a trustful relationship is damaged and/or expected performance lags, controls need to be carried out more often.

Arbitrary and unexpected controls can be a strain on trusting relationships.

Regarding your secretary, the rules are quite the same. It is, however, an important factor that your secretary has fewer standard tasks and more new or special ones and that your relationship is closer than other working relations. Therefore, your secretary expects greater confidence in her work performance, and you will have to rely on her for a confident and effective cooperation on many tasks.

E.6.   PRIVILEGE

Special positions and privileges, i.e. a preferment of persons having a similar place in company hierarchy, must be avoided because it creates jealousy and envy.

Privileges that have been earned by employees by their position in the company are generally accepted and can also be an incentive for better work performance.

General statements about sensible and motivating privileges for your secretary cannot be made here, because the respective situations at companies can be much varied. Here, individual, well-considered solutions are needed. A freshly hired, young secretary should surely not get more privileges than, e.g. your operating manager. But to a proficient, senior secretary, certain privileges can of course be given.

When granting certain privileges (the convenient parking space, flexible working hours, 1st or 2nd-class rail tickets etc. you determine indirectly, but still noticeably, position and rank of the employee in question. The measure of privileges for your secretary has to be appropriate to the rank and position among the staff you wish to assign her.

| Tip 10: |
| Privileges can show the position and |
| rank of an employee. |

E.7.   POSITIVE AND NEGATIVE FEEDBACK

Praise and reprimand should not be spontaneous, momentary expressions of feeling but sensibly deployed instruments to build up and reinforce required working methods or behaviour.

By giving praise, you reinforce required and positive working behaviour and - motivation. By doing this, you disclose also some information about yourself. You will convey your expectations and value systems, as well as the ones you require in the company. This will give employees a security regarding behaviour and focus. The more co-workers will 'witness' it, the greater and more sustained the effect of the reinforcement will be. If you give praise too often, however, the reinforcing effect on required behaviour will wear off.

It is important that the praise you give will be focused on and limited to certain concrete skills and achievements. General praise, referring to a person generally, as

19

in 'a pearl of the house' 'the pick of the bunch' or 'What would we do without her' cannot be recommended. By giving this kind of praise, you will

create in her, and also in others, a feeling of omnipotence, i.e. that the person concerned is infallible and practically cannot do wrong.

Her self-perception (the way how your secretary regards herself) and the perception of others (how you regard her performance) are often worlds apart. If you commend your secretary in a 'general' way, you will support, without exception, all her positive opinions about herself. This kind of 'false praise' is hard to correct.

Praising an employee can also be done in a 'negative' way. If your secretary had an important part in the implementation of a major project, and you mention only a little detail of her work, she and others will realize that you are dissatisfied with her work as a whole. By the targeted use of praise, much criticism can be conveyed. This 'negative' way of praising people should, however, be avoided in the interest of a constructive corporate climate.

A special commend for one or a few selected employees at a corporate function should generally be avoided, because the employees not mentioned will feel offended and depreciated, and later reactions of envy or jealousy may be hard to handle.

Reprimands, i.e. verbal or written cautions and warnings should be used if certain mistakes repeat, inappropriate working or social behaviours occur and talks or reminders had no or only insufficient effect.

Because self-perception and the perception of others often differ, it is important to reprimand not spontaneously, but only after various other measures.

Your employees will remember your positive and negative feedback better than you may think. So everything you say has great significance. This is surely a reason to consider and weigh your words carefully.

Regarding your secretary you should, if justified by practical experience, be cautious with any reprimands. Before you give a reprimand, you have many options to shape or correct the required working behaviour. If you burden the relation of confidence to

your secretary by reprimands, it often is the start of a conflictual relation or, more generally, the beginning of its end.

Tip 11:
Praise certain abilities and performance, not the person 'as such'.

E.8.   TALKING ABOUT THE RELATIONSHIP

Talking about this is not easy and not many managers or CEOs master this art. Talks about conflicts and problems should always take place in your office, so that they have an appropriate frame and the right impact. But you should avoid being pulled into lengthy discussions Your expectations must be voiced clearly. At first, criticism should be formulated in a positive way. It is better to say: 'The tasks have to be processed faster,' than 'You are working too slow.'

If the pace does not change after the first try, however, personal criticism like 'You are too slow' may be used. Much more difficult are areas for which you lack clear facts and figures about work behaviour, and gain only an impression that you want to convey to your employee. In such cases, always voice your impression with the reservation that you could be mistaken. That way, you can openly voice an impression, gain time for further checking and your employee knows that he/she is being checked on. If the working behaviour actually changes for the better, you can still admit to have been 'wrong' in your first impression.

Personal invitations for lunch or dinner are only appropriate as an incentive, not for discussing problems or criticism. Personal invitations for dinner are always perceived by the person invited and by their co-workers as a fundamental reward. The message given to co-workers could then be: 'If I have any problems with the CEO, I will receive an invitation for dinner'. That's contradictory, of course.

Protests or statements of displeasure 'on the go' have not a deep and lasting meaning. They are rather understood as an expression of a personal mood or disposition.

E.9.   ASSESSMENTS

Written assessments are an absolute necessity even if you have only few employees. Written assessments provide an opportunity to disclose to your employees how you assess them. Your employees will know about their assessment. This prevents unpleasant surprises, helps people focusing and makes the desired work behaviour and performance more transparent.

Assessments as a part of company processes provide an opportunity to illustrate, without any special occasion, the qualitative and quantitative performance, behaviour and appearance of the employee, as well as your expectations. The assessments, however, should not be handed over without commentary but be the basis for a constructive personal interview.

Talking about the assessment will be more critical for the further work performance of the respective employee than the written assessment as such.

Tip 12:
Assessments are a chance
to regularly reflect about work performance.

F.   IF THERE IS "NO CHEMISTRY"

If the relationship between you and your secretary seems irreparably damaged, it should be terminated. "Better to end with a short, sharp shock." As a rule, a dismissal will only be possible if you have the respective assessments, reprimands and warning letters fixed and substantiated in writing.

In many cases, special counselling is also helpful.

Since opposite-sex relations at least potentially contain 'explosives', they can be very complicated. Why not try a younger, male secretary who will also be up-to date in questions of information technology? But remember to provide him with the latest PC equipment to keep him happy...

Tip 13:
Better to end
with a short, sharp shock

The author
Bernd Jaenicke

Deutsch: Bernd Jaenicke studierte Volkswirtschaft, Soziologie, Völkerrecht und Pädagogik an der EFHSS Berlin, der Freien Universität Berlin und an der London School of Economics. Er ist Autor von Büchern sowie Fachbeiträgen in Publikationen deutscher Fachverlage wie beim Verlag für die Deutsche Wirtschaft, Raabe Verlag, Haufe Verlag und viele andere Verlage. Er arbeitete in Führungs- und Beratungspositionen in der freien Wirtschaft, für Non Profit Organisationen (NGOs) und als UN Diplomat bei unterschiedlichen UN-Einrichtungen (UNCTAD, IOM, UNDRO) in Jordanien, Iran, Irak, Türkei, Ruanda, England, USA und in der Schweiz.

Jaenicke lebt heute in Berlin und arbeitet als Unternehmensberater und Inhaber der Schulungs- Beratungsgesellschaft „Sprungbrett zum Erfolg" mit einem Team von 18 Mitarbeitern für die Bereiche Weiterbildung in der beruflichen und politischen Bildung sowie in den Bereichen der Unternehmens-, Personal- und Organisationsentwicklung.

Englisch: Bernd Jaenicke studied economics, sociology, international law and education at EFHSS Berlin, Freie Universität Berlin and the London School of Economics. He is the author of books as well as articles in publications of German publishing houses such as the publishing house for the German economy, Raabe Verlag, Haufe Verlag and many other publishers. He worked in leadership and consulting positions in the private sector, for non profit organizations (NGOs) and as a UN diplomat with various UN agencies (UNCTAD, IOM, UNDRO) in Jordan, Iran, Iraq, Turkey, Rwanda, England, USA and in Switzerland.

Jaenicke now lives in Berlin and works as a management consultant and owner of the training consultancy "Sprungbrett zum Erfolg, Schulungs- und Beratungsgesellschaft" with a team of 18 employees for the areas of further business training, vocational and political education as well as in the areas of corporate, personnel and organizational development.

Kontakt zu Bernd Jaenicke:
Sprungbrett zum Erfolg, Schulungs- und Beratungsgesellschaft
E-Mail: info@sprungbrettzumerfolg.de
Internet: www.sprungbrettzumerfolg.de
Tel: 030 – 66527866, Mobil: 0174 - 4894520
Link zum Autor: http://www.sprungbrettzumerfolg.de/ueber-uns/inhaber/
Link zum Autor: https://de.wikipedia.org/wiki/Bernd_Jaenicke

Bernd Jaenicke ist Autor folgender Veröffentlichungen, die bei Amazon.de und anderen Verlagen bestellt werden können:

Für Unternehmen der betrieblichen Wirtschaft und der Sozialwirtschaft

Themenreihe I: Unternehmensführung
Themenheft 1: Innovative Formen der Arbeitsorganisation,
Berlin 2018, 37 Seiten
Themenheft 2: Systematisches Beschwerdemanagement als Instrument
kundenorientierter Unternehmensführung,
Berlin 2018, 25 Seiten
Themenheft 3: Die Kundenfreundlichkeit gehört ins Unternehmenskonzept,
Berlin 2018, 39 Seiten

Themenreihe I: Unternehmensführung: Personalmanagement

Themenheft 4: Führungsstile, Berlin 2018, 27 Seiten
Themenheft 5: Zielvereinbarungsgespräche, Berlin 2018, 25 Seiten
Themenheft 6: Warum Zielvereinbarungen oft scheitern,
Berlin 2018, 25 Seiten
Themenheft 7: Das Kritikgespräch, Berlin 2019, 32 Seiten
Themenheft 8: So reduzieren Sie die Fehlzeiten Ihrer Mitarbeiter,
Berlin 2019, 26 Seiten
Themenheft 9: Bewerberauswahl, Berlin 2019, 26 Seiten
Themenheft 10: Trennungsgespräche in Unternehmen, Berlin 2019, 14Seiten

Themenreihe I: Unternehmensführung: Mitarbeiter motivieren

Themenheft 11: So motivieren Sie Ihre Mitarbeiter, Berlin 2019, 20 Seiten
Themenheft 12: Mitarbeitermotivation, betriebliche Anreize außerhalb der
Vergütungssysteme, Berlin 2019, 30 Seiten
Themenheft 13: Coaching für Ihre Mitarbeiter, Berlin 2019, 24 Seiten
Themenheft 14: Wie Sie Ihre Mitarbeiter auch in schwierigen Situationen
souverän und erfolgreich führen, Berlin 2019, 26 Seiten

Themenreihe I: Unternehmensführung: Unternehmensnachfolge

Themenheft 15: Erfolgreiche Betriebsübergabe, Berlin 2019, 26 Seiten
Themenheft 16: Unternehmensübergabe an Nachfolger: Berlin 2019, 25 Seiten
Themenheft 17: Unternehmensnachfolge aus der Sicht der Personalabteilung,
Berlin 2019, 25 Seiten

Themenreihe I: Unternehmensführung: Bankgespräche

Themenheft 18: Das Gespräch mit der Bank, Ratinggespräche zur
Unternehmensübernahme, Berlin 2019, 35 Seiten

Themenreihe I: Unternehmensführung: Konflikte und Kommunikation
Themenheft 19: Konflikte erkennen und lösen, Berlin 2019, 32 Seiten
Themenheft 20: Ich und meine Sekretärin, Unternehmenskultur,
            Berlin 2019, 29 Seiten

Themenreihe I: Unternehmensführung: Mobbing

Themenheft 21: Mobbing im Betrieb, Berlin 2019, 17 Seiten
Themenheft 22: So wehren Sie sich gegen Mobbing, Berlin 2019, 26 Seiten

Themenreihe I: Unternehmensführung: Führungskräfte und
            Management
Themenheft 23: Führungskräfte im Wandel, Berlin 2019, 28 Seiten
Themenheft 24: Management in Krisensituationen, Berlin 2019, 20 Seiten
Themenheft 25: Managementtrends, Berlin 2019, 22 Seiten

Themenreihe I: Unternehmensführung: Zeit- und Selbstmanagement

Themenheft 26: Führungskräfte unter Stress, Berlin 2019, 21 Seiten
Themenheft 27: Zeitmanagement, Berlin 2019, 25 Seiten
Themenheft 28: So präsentieren Sie Ihr Anliegen, Berlin 2019, 28 Seiten
Themenheft 29: Verhandeln wie ein Profi, Berlin 2019, 26 Seiten

Themenreihe I: Unternehmensführung: Sponsoring und Werbung
Themenheft 30: Die Bausteine eines erfolgreichen Sponsoring-Konzepts,
            Berlin 2019, 37 Seiten

Themenreihe II:
Für Unternehmen der Sozialwirtschaft (NGOs und Stiftungen)

Themenreihe II: Vereine und Stiftungen

Themenheft 1: Spender, Spenden und Spendenbriefe, Berlin 2019, 38 Seiten
Themenheft 2: Spendenbriefe und Spenderbindung, Berlin 2019, 28 Seiten
Themenheft 3: Grundlagen und Methoden des Fundraisings, Berlin 2019,
            28 Seiten
Themenheft 4: Sozial Sponsoring – Grundlagen, Muster-Sponsoringvertrag
            Berlin 2019, 32 Seiten
Themenheft 5: Die Bausteine eines Sponsoring-Konzepts, Berlin 2019,
            39 Seiten
Themenheft 6: Fundraising und Bußgeldmarketing, Berlin 2019, 34 Seiten
Themenheft 7: IT und Databasemanagement für NGOs,
            Berlin 2019, 24 Seiten
Themenheft 8: Neue Förderer, Spenderbindung, Upgrading und
            Spenderschwund, Berlin 2019, 20 Seiten
Themenheft 9: Vorstandsmitglieder, Fundraiser und ehrenamtliche Mitarbeiter,
            Berlin 2019, 20 Seiten
Themenheft 10: Turn- und Sportvereine in der Krise, Öffentlichkeitsarbeit,
            Berlin 2019, 30 Seiten

Themenheft 11: Vereinsgründung und Mustersatzung zu einem Verein,
Berlin 2019, 28 Seiten
Themenheft 12: Stiftungen: Mustersatzungen, Berlin 2019, 26 Seiten

Themenreihe III
Für Existenzgründer und Selbständige

Themenreihe III: Existenzgründung und Marketing
Themenheft 1: Existenzgründung in Deutschland, Berlin 2019, 24 Seiten
Themenheft 2: Existenzgründung von Migranten und Geflüchteten,
Berlin 2019, 24 Seiten
Themenheft 3: Existenzgründung von Kunstschaffenden
Berlin 2019, 24 Seiten
Themenheft 4: Marketing und Werbung für Existenzgründer und Selbständige
Berlin 2019, 24 Seiten

Themenreihe IV
Für das Bewerbungsmanagement und Bewerbungstraining:
Themenreihe IV: Bewerbungsmanagement
Themenheft 1: Das Bewerbungsmanagement und Bewerbungstraining,
Berlin 2019, 24 Seiten

Themenreihe V
Zum Thema Migration und Einwanderung:
Themenreihe V: Migration und Einwanderung
Themenheft 1: Fragen und Perspektiven zur Flüchtlingspolitik,
Berlin 2019, 40 Seiten
Themenheft 2: Struktur und Aufgaben der „International Organization
for Migration" (IOM), Berlin 2019, 39 Seiten
Themenheft 3: Möglichkeiten zur Steuerung der Migration,
Berlin 2019, 21 Seiten
Themenheft 4: Auf dem Weg zur neuen Heimat, Berlin 2019, 25 Seiten
Themenheft 5: Migrationsfragen nach der Eiwanderung
Berlin 2019, 40 Seiten
Themenheft 6: Migration: Gesellschaft und Werte im Wandel,
Berlin 2019, 24 Seiten
Themenheft 7: Interkulturelle Kompetenz, Berlin 2019, 24 Seiten

Themenreihe VI: English Editions
English edition 001: Me and my secretary, Berlin 2019, 27 pages
English edition 002: Customer-friendliness is a part of the corporate concept,
Berlin 2019, 34 pages
English edition 003: Employee motivation, operational rewards outside the
remuneration systems, Berlin 2019, 28 pages
English edition 004: Why target agreements often fail, Berlin 2019, 26 pages
English edition 005: Company handover to a successor, Berlin 2019, 28 pages
English edition 006: Mobbing in companies, Berlin 2019, 26 pages
English edition 007: Executives under stress, Berlin 2019, 29 pages
English edition 008: Concept of a successfull sponsorship plan, Berlin 2019,
28 pages

Themenreihe VII: Sondereditionen:

Sonderedition Bildung: Serie 001:
>Handbuch für das Qualitätsmanagements im Bereich des Bildungswesens, Berlin 2019, 120 Seiten

Sonderedition Bildung: Serie 002:
>Die Bildungs- und Beratungsangebote des Bildungsträgers: Sprungbrett zum Erfolg, Schulungs- und Beratungsgesellschaft 2019, Berlin 2019, 180 Seiten

Sonderedition Marketing: Serie 001:
>Sponsoring und Großspenderbetreuung, Berlin 2019, 255 Seiten

Sonderedition Fundraising: Serie 001:
>CRM Fundraisingsoftware OBOLUS, Spezifikation und Applikation einer Fundraisingsoftware für NGOs, praktische Anleitung für ein Pflichtenheft, Berlin 2019, 143 Seiten

Sonderedition Fundraising: Serie 002:
>Das Fundraisinglexikon von A – Z, Berlin 2019, 420 Seiten

Sonderedition Völkerrecht und internationale Beziehungen: Serie 001:
>Die internationalen Zucker-Übereinkommen von 1977 – 1984, Berlin 2019, 164 Seiten